The RV Travel Journal

THE ULTIMATE
ROAD TRIP RECORD

Sarah Cribari

ULYSSES PRESS

Published in the U.S. by:
ULYSSES PRESS
PO Box 3440
Berkeley, CA 94703
www.ulyssespress.com

ISBN: 978-1-64604-197-8
Library of Congress Control Number: 2021931513

Printed in Canada by Marquis Book Printing
10 9 8 7 6 5 4 3 2 1

Acquisitions editor: Casie Vogel
Managing editor: Claire Chun
Editor: Anne Healey
Proofreader: Renee Rutledge
Front cover design: Jake Flaherty
Interior design and layout: what!design @ whatweb.com
Images: cover © Andrii Stepaniuk/shutterstock.com; interior from shutterstock.com

This journal belongs to:

Contents

About *The RV Travel Journal*

The RV Travel Journal: The Ultimate Road Trip Record Book is your guide to logging all the details from your RV and camping trips. Whether you're a solo traveler or planning an epic family vacation, *The RV Travel Journal* helps you capture both your top memories and all the little details about your favorite (or not-so-favorite!) camping spots.

Use this journal to plan and keep a record of your RV trips. The book is split into three parts to make both preparing for and remembering your camping trips simple and easy. You can use this book in order or jump around to your favorite sections—it's really up to you!

Part 1, "Planning Your Trip," is the pre-trip strategizing section. It will help you plan meals, remember what to pack, and set your intentions for the trip. And just in case you need a bit of inspiration to figure out where to go, there's information on a few of the most popular U.S. road trips.

Part 2, "Hitting the Road!," is the travel log section. This is where you'll record your travels, including campground details and memories of each location. It's filled with prompts to help you track campsite amenities, ratings, and notes on whether you'd return to the same spot next time. There are also handy tracking logs for your favorite roadside stops and wildlife sightings, hour and mileage records, and RV and vehicle maintenance—and even some game ideas for those long drive days.

Part 3, "Trip Favorites and Memories," helps you look back on your overall favorite experiences and wrap up your thoughts on the trip. There's also space for you to plan your next big adventure!

The RV Travel Journal: The Ultimate Road Trip Record Book is the perfect keepsake of your adventures. Now let's get planning!

Our RV

RV name: ....

Type of RV: ....

RV make and model: ....

RV length: ....

RV height: ....

PART 1

Planning Your Trip

Setting Intentions for Your Trip

People take RV trips for different reasons. For some it's to spend more time with the family away from screens. For others it's to get away from everyone and be surrounded by nature while still having some of the comforts of home. Some people love the community of a large RV resort, while others crave alone time deep in the woods. Sit and think for a few moments about why you're taking this trip and what you want to get out of it. Is it to soak in the silence of a remote boondocking location by a gorgeous lake? Are you fulfilling a longtime dream of experiencing the beauty of a U.S. National Park with your children? Do you want to escape the busy city and satisfy your craving for the smell of the woods? Use the journal space below to record your thoughts and make note of what you want to accomplish on this trip. Once these things are on your mind and written down, it'll be easier to make them happen when you begin your adventure.

I want my/our RV trip to include:

Get Ready to Pack

Depending on where you're going on your trip, you'll have to remember to pack different items. Once you've planned your itinerary, check the weather at your destinations during your arrival dates so you can pack smarter and not realize you're missing important supplies (like an insulated water hose for cold weather!) halfway through the trip. There's only so much room in an RV, so everything needs to have a reason to come along. Prioritize items that can serve double duty, as well as items that make the trip more comfortable.

This packing section is split into two checklists: one for personal packing and another for more general RV packing. Use the personal packing checklist for things you would bring on any vacation—clothing, toiletries, hiking shoes, etc. The RV packing checklist is where you can list all the general items to pack, such as cleaning supplies, dishes, extra towels, water hoses, and anything else you'll need to remember to bring in the RV.

Some Handy RV Items to Pack

- ☐ First aid kit
- ☐ Emergency road kit
- ☐ Toilet paper
- ☐ Cleaning supplies
- ☐ Kitchen supplies: dishes, pots and pans, silverware, any small appliances
- ☐ Leveling blocks
- ☐ Level (if your RV doesn't have an automatic leveler)
- ☐ Drinking water hose
- ☐ Utility water hose

- ☐ Sewer hoses (gray and black) and connecters
- ☐ Camping table and chairs
- ☐ Water filter
- ☐ Vacuum, mop, or dry mop (you'd be surprised at how much dirt and sand will find its way in!)
- ☐ Bedding
- ☐ Towels
- ☐ A few books and games
- ☐ Skewers for marshmallows, hot dogs, etc.
- ☐ Trash bags

Personal Packing Checklist

(Examples: jacket, socks, hiking boots, toothbrush, etc.)

RV Packing Checklist

(Examples: bedding, towels, kitchen supplies, bikes, etc.)

Meal Planning

You've set your intentions; the RV is packed—but what are you going to eat? Hot dogs and s'mores cooked over the campfire are great, but if you're taking a longer trip, you're going to need a more balanced diet. Thankfully, even though there's not typically a ton of space, most RVs come with some type of kitchen setup. And meal planning can be a lifesaver when you need to maximize the small amount of space you do have.

If you're taking a shorter trip, planning most or all of your meals before you leave allows you to purchase the needed ingredients and make the meals ahead of time so you won't have to worry about what to cook when you're in the middle of your vacation. For those on longer trips, meal planning helps you figure out what to buy when grocery shopping so you can keep your RV stocked with the ingredients you need and not waste precious space with random food items you'll never use.

For any length of trip, you can prepare meals beforehand at home, where you may have more space. You can then freeze these meals and pull them out on your trip so you won't have to spend time on meal prep every day. After a long day of driving and getting set up at camp, thawing a frozen pot of soup is a breeze and provides a satisfying and healthy meal.

Meal-Planning Tips

○ Spend time meal planning before you leave. It's much easier to do this at home than on the road. Decide on at least a few of the meals you'll eat on the trip, and either make them ahead of time or purchase the ingredients to make them on the road.

○ Cook freezable parts of your meals at home beforehand. Making spaghetti sauce or soups at home that can be heated up on a stove or over the campfire will save time and energy on your trip.

○ Do research on your destination before you leave. Are there grocery stores nearby, or are you heading into the wilderness? If you're going to be away from civilization, be sure to include ingredients for a few extra dishes when meal planning. But even if there's a grocery store down the street from your campsite, who wants to spend time shopping for groceries when you could be outside exploring?

○ Think about ingredients that work in multiple meals. If you're planning tacos one night, why not use the rest of the tortillas for breakfast burritos? Or if you're grilling chicken, cook a few extra pieces and use them for salads, sandwiches, or a soup the next day.

○ Don't forget about snacks on the road! Be sure to bring along something to eat and drink in the car on those long drive days. Granola bars, sliced veggies, trail mix, cheese and crackers, and easy PB&J sandwiches are all low-mess snacks that travel well and can save the day when people start getting hangry. We've all been there, and a well-timed snack can turn a bad trip around.

Weekly Meal Planners

Use this template to plan your meals and snacks for your trip. If you need some ideas, take a look at page 20 for meal suggestions!

Meals for the week of ....

	Breakfast	Lunch	Dinner	Snacks
Mon				
Tues				
Wed				
Thurs				
Fri				
Sat				
Sun				

Meals for the week of ....

	Breakfast	Lunch	Dinner	Snacks
Mon				
Tues				
Wed				
Thurs				
Fri				
Sat				
Sun				

Meals for the week of ....

	Breakfast	Lunch	Dinner	Snacks
Mon				
Tues				
Wed				
Thurs				
Fri				
Sat				
Sun				

Meals for the week of ....

	Breakfast	Lunch	Dinner	Snacks
Mon				
Tues				
Wed				
Thurs				
Fri				
Sat				
Sun				

Easy Camping Meal Ideas

You want to keep things simple when planning meals for camping. Look for recipes that don't use a ton of ingredients and won't take forever to cook. There are many cookbooks and websites that share recipes meant for campfire and camp cooking, so take some time to research recipes before you leave. Campfire meals cooked in aluminum foil packets, in a Dutch oven, or on skewers make for easy and fun options. If you're looking to do more cooking inside your RV than outside, a slow cooker or instant pressure cooker is your best friend in the kitchen!

While everyone has their favorite dishes and styles of cuisine, here are a few ideas for easy camping meals to get you started. And don't forget dessert!

Breakfast

- Pancakes
- Breakfast burritos
- Egg scrambles and campfire hash
- French toast
- Avocado toast
- Premade quick breads (banana, zucchini, etc.)
- Granola
- Oatmeal
- Shakshuka
- Premade muffins
- Huevos rancheros
- Dutch oven cinnamon buns
- Ham and cheese campfire sandwiches

Lunch & Dinner

- Sandwiches
- Salads
- Campfire nachos
- Campfire baked potatoes
- Dutch oven pizza
- Camping quesadillas
- Cast iron hot dogs and beans
- Tacos
- Grilled chicken pieces
- Aluminum foil packet meals
- Grilled vegetables
- Dutch oven chili

Favorite Camping and RV Recipes

Popular U.S. Road Trip Ideas

If you're longing to take an RV trip but don't know where to start, here are a few popular road trips across the United States and Canada to help inspire you.

Historic Route 66—Illinois to California via the Southwest

Spirit of Adventure

Route 66 is a famous and historic highway that runs from Chicago, Illinois, south and west to Santa Monica, California. Established in 1926, it was considered the "Main Street of America" and called "The Mother Road" by author John Steinbeck in his novel *The Grapes of Wrath*. Today it brings up images of vintage Americana-style vacations, nostalgia for road trips, and Nat King Cole singing about where to get your kicks. While it was officially decommissioned in the mid-1980s and is no longer a main road in the United States, much of the original highway can still be explored by road trippers.

Since Route 66 was decommissioned it's not possible to stay on the historic highway the entire time. Parts of the original road are closed, converted, or no longer exist. However, there is still plenty of the classic drive to explore. The best way to road trip on Historic Route 66 is with a guidebook or map that will show you the routes you can take to stay as close to the original highway as possible.

Where: A road trip along Route 66 will take you through Illinois, Missouri, Kansas, Oklahoma, Texas, New Mexico, Arizona, and California, and is filled with iconic American roadside attractions, food, and places to stay.

Attractions: There's no shortage of activities to explore on Route 66. Some highlights include the Petrified Forest, the Mojave Desert, the Painted Desert, vintage gas stations, roadside diners, statues and art installations, and historic railroads. It's also known for its quirky roadside attractions, such as Cadillac Ranch, the Muffler Men, the world's largest rocking chair, the Blue Whale of Catoosa, and the Continental Divide. If you're looking to check another National Park off your list, the Grand Canyon is a short day trip from the route and can easily be added to your trip.

What to Expect: Driving along Historic Route 66 will take adventurers through different American landscapes, such as prairies, deserts, farmland, and mountains. You can drive this trip from east to west or from west to east. It's also very easy to take a small section of Historic Route 66 and explore that particular area during a shorter trip.

Weather: Because Historic Route 66 crosses so many states and climates, weather will vary throughout the trip. Generally, the best time to do this road trip is between March and October to avoid potentially snowy road conditions. However, some of this route goes through long stretches of desert in the Southwest, and the summer months can easily reach temperatures over 100 degrees Fahrenheit. Late spring or early fall will typically provide the best weather for the trip. Be sure to check the weather conditions all along your route to prepare.

Pacific Coast Highway—California to Washington

Towering redwood trees, seaside cliffs, and gorgeous ocean views await travelers along the Pacific Coast Highway (or PCH). This incredibly scenic road trip runs along California Highway 1 and US 101 throughout California, Oregon, and Washington. This road trip is amazing if you drive the entire route, but it's also easily split up into smaller sections. You can drive from Seattle to San Francisco, from San Francisco to San Diego, or even just from San Francisco to Los Angeles, and you'll still see amazing views along the way. Not only does the PCH pass through multiple large cities for you to explore, but it also highlights some incredible bits of nature.

Where: Driving the PCH will take you through California, Oregon, and Washington. You can either start in San Diego and head north or begin your trip in Seattle and head south. If you start in Washington and drive the route southbound, the ocean will be on the right-hand side and you'll have fantastic views of the water for much of the trip.

Attractions: While the ocean is the star of this road trip, there are many attractions and towns to visit along the way. Some of the nature-based highlights include Big Sur, Avenue of the Giants, Redwood National Park, and the elephant seals on the shores of San Simeon, all in California; and Hoh Rain Forest within Olympic National Park in Washington. Other fun places to see include cities such as Seattle, Portland, San Francisco, Santa Barbara, Santa Monica, and San Diego, and attractions like Hearst Castle, San Luis Obispo wine country, Santa Monica Pier, and the many beaches of Orange County.

What to Expect: The views may be incredible, but there are a few things RVers should keep in mind. Much of this highway runs along the ocean, and there are sharp turns and narrow bits of road to maneuver, so be careful if you have a longer or larger rig. There can also be unpredictable weather, wildfires, and even mud slides, all of which can make the roads impassable. It's best to check with the local transportation departments before you go to confirm that the highways are open.

Weather: The northern section of the Pacific Coast Highway in Washington and Oregon will be much cooler than the part that runs through southern California. The best weather in the Pacific Northwest happens during the summer and early fall. In southern California, the weather will be warm to hot for most of the year, although it can get cooler in winter. It can also be chilly along the coast with the ocean breeze. Spring is a fantastic time to take this trip since the flowers are in bloom, but you'll have more fluctuations in weather. If you're driving the entire route, pack for both cool and warm temperatures.

Florida Keys Scenic Highway—Key Largo to Key West

For those looking to escape to somewhere warm in late winter or early spring, the Florida Keys Scenic Highway may be the answer. This route is a picturesque stretch of road along U.S. Route 1 that lets travelers island-hop along Florida's archipelago, surrounded by beaches and blue-green water.

Where: The 106-mile drive connects the islands on the southern tip of Florida, from Key Largo to Key West. It takes you over the water and across multiple bridges providing gorgeous turquoise ocean views as far as you can see. There are all sorts of fun and quirky restaurants, attractions, and beaches to stop at along the way.

Attractions: Kick off your trip by taking the Overseas Highway into Key Largo, then continue down the highway to explore the towns and beaches of the Keys. Highlights include John Pennekamp Coral Reef State Park, which has opportunities for fishing, diving, kayaking, and snorkeling; the Turtle Hospital, where you can learn about the rescue and rehabilitation of endangered sea turtles; the Dolphin Research Center; and, of course, Key West. And while you can't drive there, it's easy to visit Dry Tortugas National Park by ferry or seaplane as a side trip.

What to Expect: Since this road trip is only about 100 miles long, it's drivable in a few hours. However, it's worth it to take your time and stop often to explore the area. There are so many places to swim, snorkel, dive, fish, kayak, and spend time in and on the water that you'll want to take it easy and stay for at least a few days.

Weather: The best time to visit is late winter and spring. You'll want to avoid hurricane season, which generally runs from June 1 to the end of November. And while the Keys can get hot and humid in summer, it's a beautiful, warm 70 to 80 degrees Fahrenheit in spring, so pack for the beach!

Scenic Byway 12—Utah

Scenic Byway 12 in Utah is a drive that allows travelers to experience the iconic beauty of the Southwest. Filled with red rock formations, slickrock canyons, aspen forests, quaint towns, and multiple National Parks, this trip delivers rugged scenery at every mile. It's a short drive that can be completed in a few hours, but there's so much to see that it's worth taking a few days to experience it all.

Where: This 123-mile, designated All-American Road begins in the west near Panguitch, Utah, and connects U.S. Route 89 (US 89) to Utah State Route 24 (SR-24) near Torrey, Utah, to the northeast. It also passes through two National Parks that travelers can check off their list.

Attractions: There's quite a bit to see on this drive, including two National Parks and a National Monument. Travelers can visit Bryce Canyon National Park and Capitol Reef National Park, as well as Escalante Petrified Forest State Park and Grand Staircase-Escalante National Monument. There's also Anasazi State Park and Museum, Kodachrome Basin State Park, and the Hogsback, where Scenic Byway 12 runs along the top of a steep ridge and the ground quickly falls away from the road as if you're driving along the back of a giant razorback hog. There are plenty of pull-offs along the entire route, so it's easy to pull over and safely take photos of the stunning scenery.

What to Expect: Since the road is about 123 miles, it can easily be completed in a few hours. However, the best parts of this drive are the stops along the way. Taking a few days to see everything will ensure you get the most out of this road trip. Drivers should note that the Hogsback section of road is tricky, with hairpin turns and narrow roads. It can also get windy, which may cause difficulties for larger rigs.

Weather: Spring, summer, and fall are the best times to drive this stretch of road, although it's open all year. It can get hot in the summer, but the evenings will be cooler in the spring and fall. Even though it's the desert, you'll drive through aspen and pine groves, so don't forget a jacket if you visit during the cooler months. This region gets snow in winter, and the road may close temporarily after snowstorms until it can be plowed.

Blue Ridge Parkway—Virginia to North Carolina

Blue Ridge Parkway is a beautiful drive along the Appalachian Mountains in Virginia and North Carolina. Connecting two National Parks, Blue Ridge Parkway is full of mileposts with gorgeous views and fun activities for the whole family. This scenic road trip features a historic mill, beautiful hikes, sites showcasing local history and crafts, and plenty of scenery.

Where: Blue Ridge Parkway starts at the southern part of Shenandoah National Park in Virginia and ends 469 miles later at Great Smoky Mountains National Park in North Carolina.

Attractions: There are many scenic overlooks where you can pull off and enjoy the views throughout the entire drive. Aside from stunning vistas of the mountains and colorful foliage if you visit in fall, highlights include Roanoke, Mabry Mill, the Mile-High Swinging Bridge, Mount Mitchell State Park, and Craggy Gardens. There's also a fantastic variety of hikes if you want to enjoy the region on foot as well as by RV.

What to Expect: Much of the Blue Ridge Parkway is hilly and winding, which could potentially pose problems for larger rigs. There are also several tunnels with height restrictions along the parkway that may cause issues for tall RVs. To make sure your RV will fit, measure the height of your rig and research tunnel height restrictions before you go. It's also a fairly slow drive. The speed limit maxes out at 45 miles per hour but often drops lower. With all the hills and turns along the road, that can mean slow going for RVs. But it just leaves more time for enjoying the views!

Weather: While beautiful in spring and summer, this drive really shines in fall, when the leaves on the trees start turning red and yellow. In summer the weather is mild to warm, but temperatures will start dropping in fall. Be sure to pack a jacket for cooler evenings.

Western National Parks—Yellowstone, Grand Teton, and Glacier National Parks

Some of the most beautiful and rugged parts of the United States can be found out west. If National Parks are on your bucket list, this road trip will take you to three of the most popular National Parks in the western United States: Grand Teton, Yellowstone, and Glacier National Parks. There's even the option to cross into Canada to visit Waterton Lakes National Park, a great way to extend your trip for a few extra days.

Where: Yellowstone and Grand Teton National Parks are a short drive from each other down John D. Rockefeller, Jr. Memorial Parkway in Wyoming. Start in Grand Teton National Park, which is farther south, then make your way north a few miles to Yellowstone National Park. Once you've explored those parks, head north through Montana to Glacier National Park. If you have your passport, you can also hop across the border into Canada to visit Waterton Lakes National Park in Alberta. Waterton Lakes and Glacier parks have partnered to form Waterton-Glacier International Peace Park, letting adventurers explore more of North America's incredible scenery.

Attractions: All of these National Parks deliver epic scenery and natural beauty. Within Grand Teton National Park you'll want to visit Teton Park Road, Mormon Row Historic District, Signal Mountain, Jenny Lake, and Schwabacher Landing. In Yellowstone National Park don't miss Midway Geyser Basin, Grand Prismatic Spring Overlook, Grand Canyon of the Yellowstone, and of course, Old Faithful Geyser. Once you get into Glacier National Park, Going-to-the-Sun Road is not to be skipped, along with Lake McDonald, Logan Pass, and St. Mary Lake.

What to Expect: There are multiple campgrounds inside and around the parks, but these fill up quickly, especially in summer, so be sure to make reservations well in advance. Going-to-the-Sun Road in Glacier National Park has both height and length restrictions on vehicles, so depending on the size of your rig you may have to drive this in a tow vehicle. The road also closes in winter due to snow, so if it's on your bucket list, plan to visit in late summer.

Weather: These National Parks offer visitors amazing activities and views during all seasons; however, the most popular time to visit is in the summer, when the weather is warm. While all three National Parks are open year-round, winter weather can make driving difficult, and both roads and entire sections of these parks will shut down due to bad snow or ice during the winter. Going-to-the-Sun Road in Glacier National Park typically doesn't fully open until July—weather permitting—and it closes sometime in October. If you want to drive that iconic road, aim for visiting in August or early September. Check the National Park Service website (NPS.gov) to confirm which sections of the parks are open if you'd prefer to visit during the winter. Since all these National Parks are rugged and remote, you'll be at the mercy of the weather, which can run from hot to freezing. Check the weather before you leave on your trip to get a better idea of what to pack.

Alaska Highway—British Columbia Canada to Alaska

Not for the faint of heart, the famous Alaska Highway is one of the most beautiful drives in North America. Also known as the Alcan Highway, this drive is just shy of 1,400 miles and traverses some of the more remote regions of Canada and Alaska. It's filled with wildlife sightings, stunning landscapes, and a vast wilderness not found in the lower 48 states. A road trip on the Alaska Highway is long and daunting, but it rewards travelers with incredible sights and memories of North America.

Where: The Alaska Highway begins in the northern part of British Columbia, Canada, in the town of Dawson Creek, and takes you through the Yukon Territory into Alaska. It ends in Delta Junction, Alaska, near Fairbanks.

Attractions: While the beautiful scenery and rugged landscapes are the main draw of this trip, there are plenty of activities you can enjoy along the drive. The trip begins at mile 0 in Dawson Creek, British Columbia, with the iconic Alaska Highway sign and the Alaska Highway House museum. Heading into the Yukon Territory, you can visit the famous Signpost Forest, Watson Lake, the town of Whitehorse, Kluane National Park and Reserve, and the Continental Divide. Once you cross into Alaska you'll find the official end of the highway at Delta Junction.

What to Expect: The roads range from smooth to rough, and you'll be crossing the Canada/U.S. border, so be aware of any customs and border-crossing requirements. While most of the Alaska Highway is paved, there are still frost heaves and stretches of gravel that can make driving difficult. There are also long stretches of road without gas stations, so it's best to fill up whenever you can. Limited cell phone service is also a consideration throughout the drive, so come prepared with paper maps (yes, those still exist!) and guidebooks in case your phone or GPS isn't getting a signal.

Weather: Although people drive this route year-round, summer and early fall are the best times to go. The weather is typically mild during this time of the year. Beware of going too late in the season or the weather will get significantly colder as you drive further north. The summer also provides longer days, which makes it easier to drive in the evenings. However, bring something to black out your RV windows as the extended daylight can make it difficult to sleep.

Road Trip Games

Keeping kids (and adults) occupied during those long drive days can be difficult, especially if you're trying to cut down on screen time. Here are some classic and favorite road trip games to help keep everyone's spirits up when the hours and minutes seem to drag by.

The Alphabet Game

This classic car game is still a great way to pass the time. Starting at *A* and going all the way to *Z*, the passengers in the car must find a word that starts with each letter in order using road signs, wording on trucks, license plates, or anywhere you can find writing outside of the car. To make it more difficult, implement a "no license plates" rule!

The License Plate Game

This game is especially fun if you're driving across the country. Look for license plates from different states, and keep a running list of all the states you find throughout your trip. You probably won't find all 50, but who knows? You can have passengers team up to work together or have everyone keep track of their own findings to make it a competition.

Going on a Camping Trip (Going on a Picnic)

A twist on the classic story game "Going on a Picnic," this version follows the same rules. Someone in the vehicle starts by saying, "I'm going on a camping trip and I'm going to bring..." and naming an item. The next person starts the same way, saying, "I'm going on a camping trip and I'm going to bring..." but they must name the first person's item and then add their own. The next person in line must list all the previous items in order and then add their own item, and so on. The first person to forget an item or get them out of order loses.

Silly Rules

Everyone in the car/truck/RV gets to make up a silly rule for travel days. The rule should be something ridiculous that everyone can easily do, such as "Every time we see another RV everyone has to yell 'RV buddy!'" or "Any time we cross a state line everyone has to clap." Each time one of the rules happens, the last person to catch on and participate in that rule gets a point. The person with the least points when you get to the campsite wins.

Wildlife List

Whether it's a cow lazily grazing in a field or a family of elk crossing a stream, catching a glimpse of animals you don't normally see every day is part of the fun of road tripping. Use this space to record the different types of animals that you come across on your trip.

Animal	Location

State Tracking List

Which states did you visit on your trip? Check the box for every state you drove through or stopped in. (Don't forget to check off Washington, DC, if you pass through the nation's capital!)

- ☐ Alabama
- ☐ Alaska
- ☐ Arizona
- ☐ Arkansas
- ☐ California
- ☐ Colorado
- ☐ Connecticut
- ☐ Delaware
- ☐ Florida
- ☐ Georgia
- ☐ Hawaii
- ☐ Idaho
- ☐ Illinois
- ☐ Indiana
- ☐ Iowa
- ☐ Kansas
- ☐ Kentucky
- ☐ Louisiana
- ☐ Maine
- ☐ Maryland

- ☐ Massachusetts
- ☐ Michigan
- ☐ Minnesota
- ☐ Mississippi
- ☐ Missouri
- ☐ Montana
- ☐ Nebraska
- ☐ Nevada
- ☐ New Hampshire
- ☐ New Jersey
- ☐ New Mexico
- ☐ New York
- ☐ North Carolina
- ☐ North Dakota
- ☐ Ohio
- ☐ Oklahoma
- ☐ Oregon
- ☐ Pennsylvania
- ☐ Rhode Island
- ☐ South Carolina

- ☐ South Dakota
- ☐ Tennessee
- ☐ Texas
- ☐ Utah
- ☐ Vermont
- ☐ Virginia
- ☐ Washington (state)
- ☐ Washington, DC
- ☐ West Virginia
- ☐ Wisconsin
- ☐ Wyoming

Roadside Attractions

The United States is full of quirky roadside attractions. If you're looking for a way to break up long drive days, a stop at one of these unique locations makes for a great rest and some fun photos! Road trip smartphone apps and websites can help you find attractions along your route. There are many interesting sites to visit; here are just a few examples to look out for if you pass that way on your trip.

- **Biosphere 2**–Oracle, Arizona
- **Bishop Castle**–Rye, Colorado
- **Cabazon Dinosaurs**–Cabazon, California
- **Cadillac Ranch**–Amarillo, Texas
- **Carhenge**–Alliance, Nebraska
- **Dinosaur Land**–White Post, Virginia
- **Enchanted Highway**–Regent, North Dakota
- **Future Birthplace of Captain Kirk**–Riverside, Iowa
- **Golden Driller**–Tulsa, Oklahoma
- **Hole N" The Rock**–Moab, Utah
- **International UFO Museum & Research Center**–Roswell, New Mexico
- **Jolly Green Giant**–Blue Earth, Minnesota
- **Leaning Tower of Niles**–Niles, Illinois
- **London Bridge**–Lake Havasu City, Arizona
- **Lucy the Elephant**–Margate City, New Jersey
- **Prada Marfa**–Valentine, Texas
- **Unclaimed Baggage Center**–Scottsboro, Alabama
- **Wall Drug Store**–Wall, South Dakota
- **Winchester Mystery House**–San Jose, California
- **World's Largest Garden Gnome**–Kerhonkson, New York

Favorite Roadside Stops and Attractions

U.S. National Parks

The United States is home to many beautiful National Parks that highlight the natural wonders of the country. And one of the best ways to visit the wide variety of U.S. National Parks is in an RV! The National Park System currently has 63 designated "National Park" sites across the United States and U.S. territories. These incredible locations are a wonderful way to escape the city and experience the often awe-inspiring power of nature. Many National Parks have campgrounds and RV parks nearby or even inside their boundaries, making them a favorite destination for RVers.

Use this alphabetical checklist to keep track of the National Parks that you visit on your trip.

◻ Acadia National Park—Maine

◻ Arches National Park—Utah

◻ Badlands National Park—South Dakota

◻ Big Bend National Park—Texas

◻ Biscayne National Park—Florida

◻ Black Canyon of the Gunnison National Park—Colorado

◻ Bryce Canyon National Park—Utah

◻ Canyonlands National Park—Utah

◻ Capitol Reef National Park—Utah

◻ Carlsbad Caverns National Park—New Mexico

◻ Channel Islands National Park—California

◻ Congaree National Park—South Carolina

◻ Crater Lake National Park—Oregon

- [ ] Cuyahoga Valley National Park–Ohio
- [ ] Death Valley National Park–California/Nevada
- [ ] Denali National Park–Alaska
- [ ] Dry Tortugas National Park–Florida
- [ ] Everglades National Park–Florida
- [ ] Gates of the Arctic National Park–Alaska
- [ ] Gateway Arch National Park–Missouri
- [ ] Glacier Bay National Park–Alaska
- [ ] Glacier National Park–Montana
- [ ] Grand Canyon National Park–Arizona
- [ ] Grand Teton National Park–Wyoming
- [ ] Great Basin National Park–Nevada
- [ ] Great Sand Dunes National Park–Colorado
- [ ] Great Smoky Mountains National Park–North Carolina/Tennessee
- [ ] Guadalupe Mountains National Park–Texas
- [ ] Haleakalā National Park–Hawaii
- [ ] Hawai'i Volcanoes National Park–Hawaii
- [ ] Hot Springs National Park–Arkansas
- [ ] Indiana Dunes National Park–Indiana
- [ ] Isle Royale National Park–Michigan
- [ ] Joshua Tree National Park–California
- [ ] Katmai National Park–Alaska
- [ ] Kenai Fjords National Park–Alaska
- [ ] Kings Canyon National Park–California

- ☐ Kobuk Valley National Park–Alaska
- ☐ Lake Clark National Park–Alaska
- ☐ Lassen Volcanic National Park–California
- ☐ Mammoth Cave National Park–Colorado
- ☐ Mesa Verde National Park–Colorado
- ☐ Mount Rainier National Park–Washington
- ☐ National Park of American Samoa–American Samoa
- ☐ New River Gorge National Park–West Virginia
- ☐ North Cascades National Park–Washington
- ☐ Olympic National Park–Washington
- ☐ Petrified Forest National Park–Arizona
- ☐ Pinnacles National Park–California
- ☐ Redwood National Park–California
- ☐ Rocky Mountain National Park–Colorado
- ☐ Saguaro National Park–Arizona
- ☐ Sequoia National Park–California
- ☐ Shenandoah National Park–Virginia
- ☐ Theodore Roosevelt National Park–North Dakota
- ☐ Virgin Islands National Park–U.S. Virgin Islands
- ☐ Voyageurs National Park–Minnesota
- ☐ White Sands National Park–New Mexico
- ☐ Wind Cave National Park–South Dakota
- ☐ Wrangell-St. Elias National Park–Alaska
- ☐ Yellowstone National Park–Wyoming/Montana/Idaho
- ☐ Yosemite National Park–California
- ☐ Zion National Park–Utah

Campsite Log

Dates: ....

Address/location: ....

Traveling from: .... Travel mileage: .... Time to destination: ....

Notable landmarks/sites en route: ....

Driving notes: ....

....

Campground/RV park name: .... Campsite #: ....

Phone number/website: ....

Would stay at this campground again? Y / N   Would stay at this campsite again? Y / N

Site hookups: Water ⬭   Electricity ⬭   Sewer ⬭   Dry camping ⬭   Was site level? Y / N

Site amenities: Cable ⬭   Internet ⬭   Fire pit ⬭   Grill ⬭   Picnic table ⬭

Cell signal at campsite (1 = terrible, 5 = fantastic):   1 2 3 4 5   Carrier: ....

Campground amenities: General store ⬭   Laundry ⬭   Pool ⬭   Bathrooms ⬭

          Showers ⬭   Dog park ⬭   Clubhouse ⬭   Dump station ⬭   Restaurant ⬭

Additional campsite notes (noise level, maneuverability, cost, scenery, etc.): ....

....

....

....

Weather during stay: ....

....

Nearby grocery stores and restaurants:

Nearby activities:

New friends and acquaintances:

Notes, Memories, & Mementos

Campsite Log

Dates: .... Address/location: ....

Traveling from: .... Travel mileage: .... Time to destination: ....

Notable landmarks/sites en route: ....

Driving notes: ....

....

Campground/RV park name: .... Campsite #: ....

Phone number/website: ....

Would stay at this campground again? Y / N   Would stay at this campsite again? Y / N

Site hookups: Water ⬡   Electricity ⬡   Sewer ⬡   Dry camping ⬡   Was site level? Y / N

Site amenities: Cable ⬡   Internet ⬡   Fire pit ⬡   Grill ⬡   Picnic table ⬡

Cell signal at campsite (1 = terrible, 5 = fantastic):   1 2 3 4 5   Carrier: ....

Campground amenities: General store ⬡   Laundry ⬡   Pool ⬡   Bathrooms ⬡

          Showers ⬡   Dog park ⬡   Clubhouse ⬡   Dump station ⬡   Restaurant ⬡

Additional campsite notes (noise level, maneuverability, cost, scenery, etc.):

....

....

....

Weather during stay: ....

....

Nearby grocery stores and restaurants:

Nearby activities:

New friends and acquaintances:

Notes, Memories, & Mementos

Campsite Log

Dates: .... Address/location: ....

Traveling from: .... Travel mileage: .... Time to destination: ....

Notable landmarks/sites en route: ....

Driving notes: ....

....

Campground/RV park name: .... Campsite #: ....

Phone number/website: ....

Would stay at this campground again? Y / N   Would stay at this campsite again? Y / N

Site hookups: Water ☁   Electricity ☁   Sewer ☁   Dry camping ☁   Was site level? Y / N

Site amenities: Cable ☁   Internet ☁   Fire pit ☁   Grill ☁   Picnic table ☁

Cell signal at campsite (1 = terrible, 5 = fantastic):   1 2 3 4 5   Carrier: ....

Campground amenities: General store ☁   Laundry ☁   Pool ☁   Bathrooms ☁

     Showers ☁   Dog park ☁   Clubhouse ☁   Dump station ☁   Restaurant ☁

Additional campsite notes (noise level, maneuverability, cost, scenery, etc.): ....

....

....

....

Weather during stay: ....

....

Nearby grocery stores and restaurants:

Nearby activities:

New friends and acquaintances:

Notes, Memories, & Mementos

Campsite Log

Dates: .... Address/location: ....

Traveling from: .... Travel mileage: .... Time to destination: ....

Notable landmarks/sites en route: ....

Driving notes: ....

....

Campground/RV park name: .... Campsite #: ....

Phone number/website: ....

Would stay at this campground again? Y / N   Would stay at this campsite again? Y / N

Site hookups: Water ⬡   Electricity ⬡   Sewer ⬡   Dry camping ⬡   Was site level? Y / N

Site amenities: Cable ⬡   Internet ⬡   Fire pit ⬡   Grill ⬡   Picnic table ⬡

Cell signal at campsite (1 = terrible, 5 = fantastic):   1 2 3 4 5   Carrier: ....

Campground amenities: General store ⬡   Laundry ⬡   Pool ⬡   Bathrooms ⬡

                    Showers ⬡   Dog park ⬡   Clubhouse ⬡   Dump station ⬡   Restaurant ⬡

Additional campsite notes (noise level, maneuverability, cost, scenery, etc.):

....

....

....

Weather during stay: ....

....

Nearby grocery stores and restaurants:

Nearby activities:

New friends and acquaintances:

Notes, Memories, & Mementos

Campsite Log

Dates: .... Address/location: ....

Traveling from: .... Travel mileage: .... Time to destination: ....

Notable landmarks/sites en route: ....

Driving notes: ....

....

Campground/RV park name: .... Campsite #: ....

Phone number/website: ....

Would stay at this campground again? Y / N   Would stay at this campsite again? Y / N

Site hookups: Water ⬡   Electricity ⬡   Sewer ⬡   Dry camping ⬡   Was site level? Y / N

Site amenities: Cable ⬡   Internet ⬡   Fire pit ⬡   Grill ⬡   Picnic table ⬡

Cell signal at campsite (1 = terrible, 5 = fantastic):   1 2 3 4 5   Carrier: ....

Campground amenities: General store ⬡   Laundry ⬡   Pool ⬡   Bathrooms ⬡

Showers ⬡   Dog park ⬡   Clubhouse ⬡   Dump station ⬡   Restaurant ⬡

Additional campsite notes (noise level, maneuverability, cost, scenery, etc.): ....

....

....

....

Weather during stay: ....

....

Nearby grocery stores and restaurants:

Nearby activities:

New friends and acquaintances:

Notes, Memories, & Mementos

Campsite Log

Dates: .... Address/location: ....

Traveling from: .... Travel mileage: .... Time to destination: ....

Notable landmarks/sites en route: ....

Driving notes: ....

....

....

Campground/RV park name: .... Campsite #: ....

Phone number/website: ....

Would stay at this campground again? Y / N   Would stay at this campsite again? Y / N

Site hookups: Water ☐   Electricity ☐   Sewer ☐   Dry camping ☐   Was site level? Y / N

Site amenities: Cable ☐   Internet ☐   Fire pit ☐   Grill ☐   Picnic table ☐

Cell signal at campsite (1 = terrible, 5 = fantastic):   1 2 3 4 5   Carrier: ....

Campground amenities: General store ☐   Laundry ☐   Pool ☐   Bathrooms ☐

Showers ☐   Dog park ☐   Clubhouse ☐   Dump station ☐   Restaurant ☐

Additional campsite notes (noise level, maneuverability, cost, scenery, etc.): ....

....

....

....

Weather during stay: ....

....

Nearby grocery stores and restaurants:

Nearby activities:

New friends and acquaintances:

Notes, Memories, & Mementos

Campsite Log

Dates: .... Address/location: ....

Traveling from: .... Travel mileage: .... Time to destination: ....

Notable landmarks/sites en route: ....

Driving notes: ....

....

Campground/RV park name: .... Campsite #: ....

Phone number/website: ....

Would stay at this campground again? Y / N   Would stay at this campsite again? Y / N

Site hookups: Water ⬡   Electricity ⬡   Sewer ⬡   Dry camping ⬡   Was site level? Y / N

Site amenities: Cable ⬡   Internet ⬡   Fire pit ⬡   Grill ⬡   Picnic table ⬡

Cell signal at campsite (1 = terrible, 5 = fantastic):   1 2 3 4 5   Carrier: ....

Campground amenities: General store ⬡   Laundry ⬡   Pool ⬡   Bathrooms ⬡

          Showers ⬡   Dog park ⬡   Clubhouse ⬡   Dump station ⬡   Restaurant ⬡

Additional campsite notes (noise level, maneuverability, cost, scenery, etc.): ....

....

....

....

Weather during stay: ....

....

Nearby grocery stores and restaurants:

Nearby activities:

New friends and acquaintances:

Notes, Memories, & Mementos

Campsite Log

Dates: .... Address/location: ....

Traveling from: .... Travel mileage: .... Time to destination: ....

Notable landmarks/sites en route: ....

Driving notes: ....

....

Campground/RV park name: .... Campsite #: ....

Phone number/website: ....

Would stay at this campground again? Y / N   Would stay at this campsite again? Y / N

Site hookups: Water ☐   Electricity ☐   Sewer ☐   Dry camping ☐   Was site level? Y / N

Site amenities: Cable ☐   Internet ☐   Fire pit ☐   Grill ☐   Picnic table ☐

Cell signal at campsite (1 = terrible, 5 = fantastic):   1 2 3 4 5   Carrier: ....

Campground amenities: General store ☐   Laundry ☐   Pool ☐   Bathrooms ☐

Showers ☐   Dog park ☐   Clubhouse ☐   Dump station ☐   Restaurant ☐

Additional campsite notes (noise level, maneuverability, cost, scenery, etc.):

....

....

....

Weather during stay:

....

Nearby grocery stores and restaurants:

Nearby activities:

New friends and acquaintances:

Notes, Memories, & Mementos

Campsite Log

Dates: .... Address/location: ....

Traveling from: .... Travel mileage: .... Time to destination: ....

Notable landmarks/sites en route: ....

Driving notes: ....
....
....

Campground/RV park name: .... Campsite #: ....

Phone number/website: ....

Would stay at this campground again? Y / N   Would stay at this campsite again? Y / N

Site hookups: Water ⬡   Electricity ⬡   Sewer ⬡   Dry camping ⬡   Was site level? Y / N

Site amenities: Cable ⬡   Internet ⬡   Fire pit ⬡   Grill ⬡   Picnic table ⬡

Cell signal at campsite (1 = terrible, 5 = fantastic):   1 2 3 4 5   Carrier: ....

Campground amenities: General store ⬡   Laundry ⬡   Pool ⬡   Bathrooms ⬡

          Showers ⬡   Dog park ⬡   Clubhouse ⬡   Dump station ⬡   Restaurant ⬡

Additional campsite notes (noise level, maneuverability, cost, scenery, etc.): ....
....
....
....
....

Weather during stay: ....
....

Nearby grocery stores and restaurants:

Nearby activities:

New friends and acquaintances:

Notes, Memories, & Mementos

Campsite Log

Dates: .... Address/location: ....

Traveling from: .... Travel mileage: .... Time to destination: ....

Notable landmarks/sites en route: ....

Driving notes: ....

....

Campground/RV park name: .... Campsite #: ....

Phone number/website: ....

Would stay at this campground again? Y / N   Would stay at this campsite again? Y / N

Site hookups: Water ⬭   Electricity ⬭   Sewer ⬭   Dry camping ⬭   Was site level? Y / N

Site amenities: Cable ⬭   Internet ⬭   Fire pit ⬭   Grill ⬭   Picnic table ⬭

Cell signal at campsite (1 = terrible, 5 = fantastic):   1 2 3 4 5   Carrier: ....

Campground amenities: General store ⬭   Laundry ⬭   Pool ⬭   Bathrooms ⬭

Showers ⬭   Dog park ⬭   Clubhouse ⬭   Dump station ⬭   Restaurant ⬭

Additional campsite notes (noise level, maneuverability, cost, scenery, etc.):

....

....

....

Weather during stay: ....

....

Nearby grocery stores and restaurants:

Nearby activities:

New friends and acquaintances:

Notes, Memories, & Mementos

Campsite Log

Dates: .... Address/location: ....

Traveling from: .... Travel mileage: .... Time to destination: ....

Notable landmarks/sites en route: ....

Driving notes: ....

....

Campground/RV park name: .... Campsite #: ....

Phone number/website: ....

Would stay at this campground again? Y / N   Would stay at this campsite again? Y / N

Site hookups: Water ⃝   Electricity ⃝   Sewer ⃝   Dry camping ⃝   Was site level? Y / N

Site amenities: Cable ⃝   Internet ⃝   Fire pit ⃝   Grill ⃝   Picnic table ⃝

Cell signal at campsite (1 = terrible, 5 = fantastic):   1 2 3 4 5   Carrier: ....

Campground amenities: General store ⃝   Laundry ⃝   Pool ⃝   Bathrooms ⃝

Showers ⃝   Dog park ⃝   Clubhouse ⃝   Dump station ⃝   Restaurant ⃝

Additional campsite notes (noise level, maneuverability, cost, scenery, etc.): ....

....

....

....

Weather during stay: ....

....

Nearby grocery stores and restaurants:

Nearby activities:

New friends and acquaintances:

Notes, Memories, & Mementos

Campsite Log

Dates: .... Address/location: ....

Traveling from: .... Travel mileage: .... Time to destination: ....

Notable landmarks/sites en route: ....

Driving notes: ....

....

Campground/RV park name: .... Campsite #: ....

Phone number/website: ....

Would stay at this campground again? Y / N   Would stay at this campsite again? Y / N

Site hookups: Water ☐   Electricity ☐   Sewer ☐   Dry camping ☐   Was site level? Y / N

Site amenities: Cable ☐   Internet ☐   Fire pit ☐   Grill ☐   Picnic table ☐

Cell signal at campsite (1 = terrible, 5 = fantastic):   1   2   3   4   5   Carrier: ....

Campground amenities: General store ☐   Laundry ☐   Pool ☐   Bathrooms ☐

          Showers ☐   Dog park ☐   Clubhouse ☐   Dump station ☐   Restaurant ☐

Additional campsite notes (noise level, maneuverability, cost, scenery, etc.): ....

....

....

....

Weather during stay: ....

....

Nearby grocery stores and restaurants:

Nearby activities:

New friends and acquaintances:

Notes, Memories, & Mementos

Campsite Log

Dates: .... Address/location: ....

Traveling from: .... Travel mileage: .... Time to destination: ....

Notable landmarks/sites en route: ....

Driving notes: ....

....

Campground/RV park name: .... Campsite #: ....

Phone number/website: ....

Would stay at this campground again? Y / N   Would stay at this campsite again? Y / N

Site hookups: Water ⬡   Electricity ⬡   Sewer ⬡   Dry camping ⬡   Was site level? Y / N

Site amenities: Cable ⬡   Internet ⬡   Fire pit ⬡   Grill ⬡   Picnic table ⬡

Cell signal at campsite (1 = terrible, 5 = fantastic):   1 2 3 4 5   Carrier: ....

Campground amenities: General store ⬡   Laundry ⬡   Pool ⬡   Bathrooms ⬡

         Showers ⬡   Dog park ⬡   Clubhouse ⬡   Dump station ⬡   Restaurant ⬡

Additional campsite notes (noise level, maneuverability, cost, scenery, etc.): ....

....

....

....

Weather during stay: ....

....

Nearby grocery stores and restaurants:

Nearby activities:

New friends and acquaintances:

Notes, Memories, & Mementos

Campsite Log

Dates: .... Address/location: ....

Traveling from: .... Travel mileage: .... Time to destination: ....

Notable landmarks/sites en route: ....

Driving notes: ....

....

Campground/RV park name: .... Campsite #: ....

Phone number/website: ....

Would stay at this campground again? Y / N   Would stay at this campsite again? Y / N

Site hookups: Water ⬡   Electricity ⬡   Sewer ⬡   Dry camping ⬡   Was site level? Y / N

Site amenities: Cable ⬡   Internet ⬡   Fire pit ⬡   Grill ⬡   Picnic table ⬡

Cell signal at campsite (1 = terrible, 5 = fantastic):   1 2 3 4 5   Carrier: ....

Campground amenities: General store ⬡   Laundry ⬡   Pool ⬡   Bathrooms ⬡

Showers ⬡   Dog park ⬡   Clubhouse ⬡   Dump station ⬡   Restaurant ⬡

Additional campsite notes (noise level, maneuverability, cost, scenery, etc.): ....

....

....

....

Weather during stay: ....

....

Nearby grocery stores and restaurants:

Nearby activities:

New friends and acquaintances:

Notes, Memories, & Mementos

Campsite Log

Dates: .... Address/location: ....

Traveling from: .... Travel mileage: .... Time to destination: ....

Notable landmarks/sites en route: ....

Driving notes: ....

....

Campground/RV park name: .... Campsite #: ....

Phone number/website: ....

Would stay at this campground again? Y / N   Would stay at this campsite again? Y / N

Site hookups: Water ⬭   Electricity ⬭   Sewer ⬭   Dry camping ⬭   Was site level? Y / N

Site amenities: Cable ⬭   Internet ⬭   Fire pit ⬭   Grill ⬭   Picnic table ⬭

Cell signal at campsite (1 = terrible, 5 = fantastic):   1 2 3 4 5   Carrier: ....

Campground amenities: General store ⬭   Laundry ⬭   Pool ⬭   Bathrooms ⬭

Showers ⬭   Dog park ⬭   Clubhouse ⬭   Dump station ⬭   Restaurant ⬭

Additional campsite notes (noise level, maneuverability, cost, scenery, etc.): ....

....

....

....

Weather during stay: ....

....

Nearby grocery stores and restaurants:

Nearby activities:

New friends and acquaintances:

Notes, Memories, & Mementos

Campsite Log

Dates: .... Address/location: ....

Traveling from: .... Travel mileage: .... Time to destination: ....

Notable landmarks/sites en route: ....

Driving notes: ....

....

Campground/RV park name: .... Campsite #: ....

Phone number/website: ....

Would stay at this campground again? Y / N   Would stay at this campsite again? Y / N

Site hookups: Water ⬡   Electricity ⬡   Sewer ⬡   Dry camping ⬡   Was site level? Y / N

Site amenities: Cable ⬡   Internet ⬡   Fire pit ⬡   Grill ⬡   Picnic table ⬡

Cell signal at campsite (1 = terrible, 5 = fantastic):   1 2 3 4 5   Carrier: ....

Campground amenities: General store ⬡   Laundry ⬡   Pool ⬡   Bathrooms ⬡

              Showers ⬡   Dog park ⬡   Clubhouse ⬡   Dump station ⬡   Restaurant ⬡

Additional campsite notes (noise level, maneuverability, cost, scenery, etc.): ....

....

....

....

Weather during stay: ....

....

Nearby grocery stores and restaurants:

Nearby activities:

New friends and acquaintances:

Notes, Memories, & Mementos

Campsite Log

Dates: .... Address/location: ....

Traveling from: .... Travel mileage: .... Time to destination: ....

Notable landmarks/sites en route: ....

Driving notes: ....

....

Campground/RV park name: .... Campsite #: ....

Phone number/website: ....

Would stay at this campground again? Y / N   Would stay at this campsite again? Y / N

Site hookups: Water ⬡   Electricity ⬡   Sewer ⬡   Dry camping ⬡   Was site level? Y / N

Site amenities: Cable ⬡   Internet ⬡   Fire pit ⬡   Grill ⬡   Picnic table ⬡

Cell signal at campsite (1 = terrible, 5 = fantastic):   1 2 3 4 5   Carrier: ....

Campground amenities: General store ⬡   Laundry ⬡   Pool ⬡   Bathrooms ⬡

          Showers ⬡   Dog park ⬡   Clubhouse ⬡   Dump station ⬡   Restaurant ⬡

Additional campsite notes (noise level, maneuverability, cost, scenery, etc.): ....

....

....

....

Weather during stay: ....

....

Nearby grocery stores and restaurants:

Nearby activities:

New friends and acquaintances:

Notes, Memories, & Mementos

Campsite Log

Dates: .... Address/location: ....

Traveling from: .... Travel mileage: .... Time to destination: ....

Notable landmarks/sites en route: ....

Driving notes: ....

....

Campground/RV park name: .... Campsite #: ....

Phone number/website: ....

Would stay at this campground again? Y / N   Would stay at this campsite again? Y / N

Site hookups: Water ⬭   Electricity ⬭   Sewer ⬭   Dry camping ⬭   Was site level?   Y / N

Site amenities: Cable ⬭   Internet ⬭   Fire pit ⬭   Grill ⬭   Picnic table ⬭

Cell signal at campsite (1 = terrible, 5 = fantastic):   1 2 3 4 5   Carrier: ....

Campground amenities: General store ⬭   Laundry ⬭   Pool ⬭   Bathrooms ⬭

Showers ⬭   Dog park ⬭   Clubhouse ⬭   Dump station ⬭   Restaurant ⬭

Additional campsite notes (noise level, maneuverability, cost, scenery, etc.):

....

....

....

Weather during stay: ....

Nearby grocery stores and restaurants:

Nearby activities:

New friends and acquaintances:

Notes, Memories, & Mementos

Campsite Log

Dates: .... Address/location: ....

Traveling from: .... Travel mileage: .... Time to destination: ....

Notable landmarks/sites en route: ....

Driving notes: ....

....

Campground/RV park name: .... Campsite #: ....

Phone number/website: ....

Would stay at this campground again? Y / N   Would stay at this campsite again? Y / N

Site hookups: Water ☐   Electricity ☐   Sewer ☐   Dry camping ☐   Was site level? Y / N

Site amenities: Cable ☐   Internet ☐   Fire pit ☐   Grill ☐   Picnic table ☐

Cell signal at campsite (1 = terrible, 5 = fantastic):   1 2 3 4 5   Carrier: ....

Campground amenities: General store ☐   Laundry ☐   Pool ☐   Bathrooms ☐

           Showers ☐   Dog park ☐   Clubhouse ☐   Dump station ☐   Restaurant ☐

Additional campsite notes (noise level, maneuverability, cost, scenery, etc.): ....

....

....

....

Weather during stay: ....

....

Nearby grocery stores and restaurants:

Nearby activities:

New friends and acquaintances:

Notes, Memories, & Mementos

Campsite Log

Dates: .... Address/location: ....

Traveling from: .... Travel mileage: .... Time to destination: ....

Notable landmarks/sites en route: ....

Driving notes: ....

....

Campground/RV park name: .... Campsite #: ....

Phone number/website: ....

Would stay at this campground again? Y / N   Would stay at this campsite again? Y / N

Site hookups: Water ⬭   Electricity ⬭   Sewer ⬭   Dry camping ⬭   Was site level? Y / N

Site amenities: Cable ⬭   Internet ⬭   Fire pit ⬭   Grill ⬭   Picnic table ⬭

Cell signal at campsite (1 = terrible, 5 = fantastic):   1 2 3 4 5   Carrier: ....

Campground amenities: General store ⬭   Laundry ⬭   Pool ⬭   Bathrooms ⬭

Showers ⬭   Dog park ⬭   Clubhouse ⬭   Dump station ⬭   Restaurant ⬭

Additional campsite notes (noise level, maneuverability, cost, scenery, etc.):

....

....

....

Weather during stay:

....

Nearby grocery stores and restaurants:

Nearby activities:

New friends and acquaintances:

Notes, Memories, & Mementos

Campsite Log

Dates: .... Address/location: ....

Traveling from: .... Travel mileage: .... Time to destination: ....

Notable landmarks/sites en route: ....

Driving notes: ....

....

Campground/RV park name: .... Campsite #: ....

Phone number/website: ....

Would stay at this campground again? Y / N   Would stay at this campsite again? Y / N

Site hookups: Water ☁   Electricity ☁   Sewer ☁   Dry camping ☁   Was site level? Y / N

Site amenities: Cable ☁   Internet ☁   Fire pit ☁   Grill ☁   Picnic table ☁

Cell signal at campsite (1 = terrible, 5 = fantastic):   1 2 3 4 5   Carrier: ....

Campground amenities: General store ☁   Laundry ☁   Pool ☁   Bathrooms ☁

          Showers ☁   Dog park ☁   Clubhouse ☁   Dump station ☁   Restaurant ☁

Additional campsite notes (noise level, maneuverability, cost, scenery, etc.): ....

....

....

....

Weather during stay: ....

....

Nearby grocery stores and restaurants:

Nearby activities:

New friends and acquaintances:

Notes, Memories, & Mementos

Campsite Log

Dates: .... Address/location: ....

Traveling from: .... Travel mileage: .... Time to destination: ....

Notable landmarks/sites en route: ....

Driving notes: ....

....

Campground/RV park name: .... Campsite #: ....

Phone number/website: ....

Would stay at this campground again? Y / N   Would stay at this campsite again? Y / N

Site hookups: Water ☁   Electricity ☁   Sewer ☁   Dry camping ☁   Was site level? Y / N

Site amenities: Cable ☁   Internet ☁   Fire pit ☁   Grill ☁   Picnic table ☁

Cell signal at campsite (1 = terrible, 5 = fantastic):   1 2 3 4 5   Carrier: ....

Campground amenities: General store ☁   Laundry ☁   Pool ☁   Bathrooms ☁

Showers ☁   Dog park ☁   Clubhouse ☁   Dump station ☁   Restaurant ☁

Additional campsite notes (noise level, maneuverability, cost, scenery, etc.):

....

....

....

....

Weather during stay: ....

....

Nearby grocery stores and restaurants:

....

Nearby activities:

....

New friends and acquaintances:

....

Notes, Memories, & Mementos

....

....

....

....

....

....

....

....

....

....

Campsite Log

Dates: .... Address/location: ....

Traveling from: .... Travel mileage: .... Time to destination: ....

Notable landmarks/sites en route: ....

Driving notes: ....

....

Campground/RV park name: .... Campsite #: ....

Phone number/website: ....

Would stay at this campground again? Y / N   Would stay at this campsite again? Y / N

Site hookups: Water ⬡   Electricity ⬡   Sewer ⬡   Dry camping ⬡   Was site level? Y / N

Site amenities: Cable ⬡   Internet ⬡   Fire pit ⬡   Grill ⬡   Picnic table ⬡

Cell signal at campsite (1 = terrible, 5 = fantastic):   1 2 3 4 5   Carrier: ....

Campground amenities: General store ⬡   Laundry ⬡   Pool ⬡   Bathrooms ⬡

          Showers ⬡   Dog park ⬡   Clubhouse ⬡   Dump station ⬡   Restaurant ⬡

Additional campsite notes (noise level, maneuverability, cost, scenery, etc.): ....

....

....

Weather during stay: ....

....

Nearby grocery stores and restaurants:

Nearby activities:

New friends and acquaintances:

Notes, Memories, & Mementos

Campsite Log

Dates: .... Address/location: ....

Traveling from: .... Travel mileage: .... Time to destination: ....

Notable landmarks/sites en route: ....

Driving notes: ....

....

Campground/RV park name: .... Campsite #: ....

Phone number/website: ....

Would stay at this campground again? Y / N   Would stay at this campsite again? Y / N

Site hookups: Water ▢   Electricity ▢   Sewer ▢   Dry camping ▢   Was site level? Y / N

Site amenities: Cable ▢   Internet ▢   Fire pit ▢   Grill ▢   Picnic table ▢

Cell signal at campsite (1 = terrible, 5 = fantastic):   1 2 3 4 5   Carrier: ....

Campground amenities: General store ▢   Laundry ▢   Pool ▢   Bathrooms ▢

            Showers ▢   Dog park ▢   Clubhouse ▢   Dump station ▢   Restaurant ▢

Additional campsite notes (noise level, maneuverability, cost, scenery, etc.): ....

....

....

....

Weather during stay: ....

....

Nearby grocery stores and restaurants:

Nearby activities:

New friends and acquaintances:

Notes, Memories, & Mementos

Campsite Log

Dates: .... Address/location: ....

Traveling from: .... Travel mileage: .... Time to destination: ....

Notable landmarks/sites en route: ....

Driving notes: ....

....

Campground/RV park name: .... Campsite #: ....

Phone number/website: ....

Would stay at this campground again? Y / N   Would stay at this campsite again? Y / N

Site hookups: Water ☐   Electricity ☐   Sewer ☐   Dry camping ☐   Was site level? Y / N

Site amenities: Cable ☐   Internet ☐   Fire pit ☐   Grill ☐   Picnic table ☐

Cell signal at campsite (1 = terrible, 5 = fantastic):   1 2 3 4 5   Carrier: ....

Campground amenities: General store ☐   Laundry ☐   Pool ☐   Bathrooms ☐

          Showers ☐   Dog park ☐   Clubhouse ☐   Dump station ☐   Restaurant ☐

Additional campsite notes (noise level, maneuverability, cost, scenery, etc.): ....

....

....

....

Weather during stay: ....

....

Nearby grocery stores and restaurants:

Nearby activities:

New friends and acquaintances:

Notes, Memories, & Mementos

Campsite Log

Dates: .... Address/location: ....

Traveling from: .... Travel mileage: .... Time to destination: ....

Notable landmarks/sites en route: ....

Driving notes: ....

....

Campground/RV park name: .... Campsite #: ....

Phone number/website: ....

Would stay at this campground again? Y / N   Would stay at this campsite again? Y / N

Site hookups: Water ⬯   Electricity ⬯   Sewer ⬯   Dry camping ⬯   Was site level? Y / N

Site amenities: Cable ⬯   Internet ⬯   Fire pit ⬯   Grill ⬯   Picnic table ⬯

Cell signal at campsite (1 = terrible, 5 = fantastic):   1 2 3 4 5   Carrier: ....

Campground amenities: General store ⬯   Laundry ⬯   Pool ⬯   Bathrooms ⬯

Showers ⬯   Dog park ⬯   Clubhouse ⬯   Dump station ⬯   Restaurant ⬯

Additional campsite notes (noise level, maneuverability, cost, scenery, etc.): ....

....

....

Weather during stay: ....

....

Nearby grocery stores and restaurants:

Nearby activities:

New friends and acquaintances:

Notes, Memories, & Mementos

Campsite Log

Dates: .... Address/location: ....

Traveling from: .... Travel mileage: .... Time to destination: ....

Notable landmarks/sites en route: ....

Driving notes: ....

....

Campground/RV park name: .... Campsite #: ....

Phone number/website: ....

Would stay at this campground again? Y / N   Would stay at this campsite again? Y / N

Site hookups: Water ☐   Electricity ☐   Sewer ☐   Dry camping ☐   Was site level? Y / N

Site amenities: Cable ☐   Internet ☐   Fire pit ☐   Grill ☐   Picnic table ☐

Cell signal at campsite (1 = terrible, 5 = fantastic):   1 2 3 4 5   Carrier: ....

Campground amenities: General store ☐   Laundry ☐   Pool ☐   Bathrooms ☐

          Showers ☐   Dog park ☐   Clubhouse ☐   Dump station ☐   Restaurant ☐

Additional campsite notes (noise level, maneuverability, cost, scenery, etc.): ....

....

....

....

Weather during stay: ....

....

Nearby grocery stores and restaurants:

Nearby activities:

New friends and acquaintances:

Notes, Memories, & Mementos

Campsite Log

Dates: .... Address/location: ....

Traveling from: .... Travel mileage: .... Time to destination: ....

Notable landmarks/sites en route: ....

Driving notes: ....

....

Campground/RV park name: .... Campsite #: ....

Phone number/website: ....

Would stay at this campground again? Y / N   Would stay at this campsite again? Y / N

Site hookups: Water ⬭   Electricity ⬭   Sewer ⬭   Dry camping ⬭   Was site level? Y / N

Site amenities: Cable ⬭   Internet ⬭   Fire pit ⬭   Grill ⬭   Picnic table ⬭

Cell signal at campsite (1 = terrible, 5 = fantastic):   1 2 3 4 5   Carrier: ....

Campground amenities: General store ⬭   Laundry ⬭   Pool ⬭   Bathrooms ⬭

          Showers ⬭   Dog park ⬭   Clubhouse ⬭   Dump station ⬭   Restaurant ⬭

Additional campsite notes (noise level, maneuverability, cost, scenery, etc.): ....

....

....

....

Weather during stay: ....

....

Nearby grocery stores and restaurants:

Nearby activities:

New friends and acquaintances:

Notes, Memories, & Mementos

Campsite Log

Dates: .... Address/location: ....

Traveling from: .... Travel mileage: .... Time to destination: ....

Notable landmarks/sites en route: ....

Driving notes: ....

....

Campground/RV park name: .... Campsite #: ....

Phone number/website: ....

Would stay at this campground again? Y / N   Would stay at this campsite again? Y / N

Site hookups: Water ⬭   Electricity ⬭   Sewer ⬭   Dry camping ⬭   Was site level? Y / N

Site amenities: Cable ⬭   Internet ⬭   Fire pit ⬭   Grill ⬭   Picnic table ⬭

Cell signal at campsite (1 = terrible, 5 = fantastic):   1 2 3 4 5   Carrier: ....

Campground amenities: General store ⬭   Laundry ⬭   Pool ⬭   Bathrooms ⬭

Showers ⬭   Dog park ⬭   Clubhouse ⬭   Dump station ⬭   Restaurant ⬭

Additional campsite notes (noise level, maneuverability, cost, scenery, etc.): ....

....

....

....

Weather during stay: ....

....

Nearby grocery stores and restaurants:

Nearby activities:

New friends and acquaintances:

Notes, Memories, & Mementos

Campsite Log

Dates: .... Address/location: ....

Traveling from: .... Travel mileage: .... Time to destination: ....

Notable landmarks/sites en route: ....

Driving notes: ....

....

Campground/RV park name: .... Campsite #: ....

Phone number/website: ....

Would stay at this campground again? Y / N   Would stay at this campsite again? Y / N

Site hookups: Water ⬭   Electricity ⬭   Sewer ⬭   Dry camping ⬭   Was site level? Y / N

Site amenities: Cable ⬭   Internet ⬭   Fire pit ⬭   Grill ⬭   Picnic table ⬭

Cell signal at campsite (1 = terrible, 5 = fantastic):   1 2 3 4 5   Carrier: ....

Campground amenities: General store ⬭   Laundry ⬭   Pool ⬭   Bathrooms ⬭

Showers ⬭   Dog park ⬭   Clubhouse ⬭   Dump station ⬭   Restaurant ⬭

Additional campsite notes (noise level, maneuverability, cost, scenery, etc.): ....

....

....

....

Weather during stay: ....

....

Nearby grocery stores and restaurants:

Nearby activities:

New friends and acquaintances:

Notes, Memories, & Mementos

Campsite Log

Dates: .... Address/location: ....

Traveling from: .... Travel mileage: .... Time to destination: ....

Notable landmarks/sites en route: ....

Driving notes: ....

....

Campground/RV park name: .... Campsite #: ....

Phone number/website: ....

Would stay at this campground again? Y / N   Would stay at this campsite again? Y / N

Site hookups: Water ⬭   Electricity ⬭   Sewer ⬭   Dry camping ⬭   Was site level? Y / N

Site amenities: Cable ⬭   Internet ⬭   Fire pit ⬭   Grill ⬭   Picnic table ⬭

Cell signal at campsite (1 = terrible, 5 = fantastic):   1 2 3 4 5   Carrier: ....

Campground amenities: General store ⬭   Laundry ⬭   Pool ⬭   Bathrooms ⬭

          Showers ⬭   Dog park ⬭   Clubhouse ⬭   Dump station ⬭   Restaurant ⬭

Additional campsite notes (noise level, maneuverability, cost, scenery, etc.): ....

....

....

....

Weather during stay: ....

....

Nearby grocery stores and restaurants:

Nearby activities:

New friends and acquaintances:

Notes, Memories, & Mementos

Campsite Log

Dates: .... Address/location: ....

Traveling from: .... Travel mileage: .... Time to destination: ....

Notable landmarks/sites en route: ....

Driving notes: ....

....

Campground/RV park name: .... Campsite #: ....

Phone number/website: ....

Would stay at this campground again? Y / N   Would stay at this campsite again? Y / N

Site hookups: Water ☁   Electricity ☁   Sewer ☁   Dry camping ☁   Was site level? Y / N

Site amenities: Cable ☁   Internet ☁   Fire pit ☁   Grill ☁   Picnic table ☁

Cell signal at campsite (1 = terrible, 5 = fantastic): 1 2 3 4 5   Carrier: ....

Campground amenities: General store ☁   Laundry ☁   Pool ☁   Bathrooms ☁

Showers ☁   Dog park ☁   Clubhouse ☁   Dump station ☁   Restaurant ☁

Additional campsite notes (noise level, maneuverability, cost, scenery, etc.): ....

....

....

Weather during stay: ....

....

Nearby grocery stores and restaurants:

Nearby activities:

New friends and acquaintances:

Notes, Memories, & Mementos

Campsite Log

Dates: .... Address/location: ....

Traveling from: .... Travel mileage: .... Time to destination: ....

Notable landmarks/sites en route: ....

Driving notes: ....

....

Campground/RV park name: .... Campsite #: ....

Phone number/website: ....

Would stay at this campground again? Y / N   Would stay at this campsite again? Y / N

Site hookups: Water ⬭   Electricity ⬭   Sewer ⬭   Dry camping ⬭   Was site level? Y / N

Site amenities: Cable ⬭   Internet ⬭   Fire pit ⬭   Grill ⬭   Picnic table ⬭

Cell signal at campsite (1 = terrible, 5 = fantastic):   1 2 3 4 5   Carrier: ....

Campground amenities: General store ⬭   Laundry ⬭   Pool ⬭   Bathrooms ⬭

Showers ⬭   Dog park ⬭   Clubhouse ⬭   Dump station ⬭   Restaurant ⬭

Additional campsite notes (noise level, maneuverability, cost, scenery, etc.): ....

....

....

....

Weather during stay: ....

....

Nearby grocery stores and restaurants:

Nearby activities:

New friends and acquaintances:

Notes, Memories, & Mementos

Campsite Log

Dates: .... Address/location: ....

Traveling from: .... Travel mileage: .... Time to destination: ....

Notable landmarks/sites en route: ....

Driving notes: ....

....

Campground/RV park name: .... Campsite #: ....

Phone number/website: ....

Would stay at this campground again? Y / N   Would stay at this campsite again? Y / N

Site hookups: Water ⬭   Electricity ⬭   Sewer ⬭   Dry camping ⬭   Was site level? Y / N

Site amenities: Cable ⬭   Internet ⬭   Fire pit ⬭   Grill ⬭   Picnic table ⬭

Cell signal at campsite (1 = terrible, 5 = fantastic):   1 2 3 4 5   Carrier: ....

Campground amenities: General store ⬭   Laundry ⬭   Pool ⬭   Bathrooms ⬭

         Showers ⬭   Dog park ⬭   Clubhouse ⬭   Dump station ⬭   Restaurant ⬭

Additional campsite notes (noise level, maneuverability, cost, scenery, etc.): ....

....

....

....

Weather during stay: ....

....

Nearby grocery stores and restaurants:

....

....

Nearby activities:

....

....

New friends and acquaintances:

....

....

Notes, Memories, & Mementos

....

....

....

....

....

....

....

....

....

....

Campsite Log

Dates: .... Address/location: ....

Traveling from: .... Travel mileage: .... Time to destination: ....

Notable landmarks/sites en route: ....

Driving notes: ....

....

Campground/RV park name: .... Campsite #: ....

Phone number/website: ....

Would stay at this campground again? Y / N   Would stay at this campsite again? Y / N

Site hookups: Water ⬡   Electricity ⬡   Sewer ⬡   Dry camping ⬡   Was site level? Y / N

Site amenities: Cable ⬡   Internet ⬡   Fire pit ⬡   Grill ⬡   Picnic table ⬡

Cell signal at campsite (1 = terrible, 5 = fantastic):   1 2 3 4 5   Carrier: ....

Campground amenities: General store ⬡   Laundry ⬡   Pool ⬡   Bathrooms ⬡

Showers ⬡   Dog park ⬡   Clubhouse ⬡   Dump station ⬡   Restaurant ⬡

Additional campsite notes (noise level, maneuverability, cost, scenery, etc.): ....

....

....

....

Weather during stay: ....

....

Nearby grocery stores and restaurants:

Nearby activities:

New friends and acquaintances:

Notes, Memories, & Mementos

Campsite Log

Dates: .... Address/location: ....

Traveling from: .... Travel mileage: .... Time to destination: ....

Notable landmarks/sites en route: ....

Driving notes: ....

....

Campground/RV park name: .... Campsite #: ....

Phone number/website: ....

Would stay at this campground again? Y / N   Would stay at this campsite again? Y / N

Site hookups: Water ◯   Electricity ◯   Sewer ◯   Dry camping ◯   Was site level? Y / N

Site amenities: Cable ◯   Internet ◯   Fire pit ◯   Grill ◯   Picnic table ◯

Cell signal at campsite (1 = terrible, 5 = fantastic):   1 2 3 4 5   Carrier: ....

Campground amenities: General store ◯   Laundry ◯   Pool ◯   Bathrooms ◯

Showers ◯   Dog park ◯   Clubhouse ◯   Dump station ◯   Restaurant ◯

Additional campsite notes (noise level, maneuverability, cost, scenery, etc.): ....

....

....

Weather during stay: ....

....

Nearby grocery stores and restaurants:

Nearby activities:

New friends and acquaintances:

Notes, Memories, & Mementos

Campsite Log

Dates: .... Address/location: ....

Traveling from: .... Travel mileage: .... Time to destination: ....

Notable landmarks/sites en route: ....

Driving notes: ....

....

Campground/RV park name: .... Campsite #: ....

Phone number/website: ....

Would stay at this campground again? Y / N   Would stay at this campsite again? Y / N

Site hookups: Water ⬡   Electricity ⬡   Sewer ⬡   Dry camping ⬡   Was site level? Y / N

Site amenities: Cable ⬡   Internet ⬡   Fire pit ⬡   Grill ⬡   Picnic table ⬡

Cell signal at campsite (1 = terrible, 5 = fantastic):   1 2 3 4 5   Carrier: ....

Campground amenities: General store ⬡   Laundry ⬡   Pool ⬡   Bathrooms ⬡

          Showers ⬡   Dog park ⬡   Clubhouse ⬡   Dump station ⬡   Restaurant ⬡

Additional campsite notes (noise level, maneuverability, cost, scenery, etc.): ....

....

....

....

Weather during stay: ....

....

Nearby grocery stores and restaurants:

Nearby activities:

New friends and acquaintances:

Notes, Memories, & Mementos

Campsite Log

Dates: .... Address/location: ....

Traveling from: .... Travel mileage: .... Time to destination: ....

Notable landmarks/sites en route: ....

Driving notes: ....

....

Campground/RV park name: .... Campsite #: ....

Phone number/website: ....

Would stay at this campground again? Y / N   Would stay at this campsite again? Y / N

Site hookups: Water ⬡   Electricity ⬡   Sewer ⬡   Dry camping ⬡   Was site level? Y / N

Site amenities: Cable ⬡   Internet ⬡   Fire pit ⬡   Grill ⬡   Picnic table ⬡

Cell signal at campsite (1 = terrible, 5 = fantastic):   1 2 3 4 5   Carrier: ....

Campground amenities: General store ⬡   Laundry ⬡   Pool ⬡   Bathrooms ⬡

Showers ⬡   Dog park ⬡   Clubhouse ⬡   Dump station ⬡   Restaurant ⬡

Additional campsite notes (noise level, maneuverability, cost, scenery, etc.): ....

....

....

....

Weather during stay: ....

....

Nearby grocery stores and restaurants:

Nearby activities:

New friends and acquaintances:

Notes, Memories, & Mementos

Campsite Log

Dates: .... Address/location: ....

Traveling from: .... Travel mileage: .... Time to destination: ....

Notable landmarks/sites en route: ....

Driving notes: ....
....

Campground/RV park name: .... Campsite #: ....

Phone number/website: ....

Would stay at this campground again? Y / N   Would stay at this campsite again? Y / N

Site hookups: Water ⬭   Electricity ⬭   Sewer ⬭   Dry camping ⬭   Was site level? Y / N

Site amenities: Cable ⬭   Internet ⬭   Fire pit ⬭   Grill ⬭   Picnic table ⬭

Cell signal at campsite (1 = terrible, 5 = fantastic):   1 2 3 4 5   Carrier: ....

Campground amenities: General store ⬭   Laundry ⬭   Pool ⬭   Bathrooms ⬭

Showers ⬭   Dog park ⬭   Clubhouse ⬭   Dump station ⬭   Restaurant ⬭

Additional campsite notes (noise level, maneuverability, cost, scenery, etc.): ....
....
....
....

Weather during stay: ....
....

Nearby grocery stores and restaurants:

Nearby activities:

New friends and acquaintances:

Notes, Memories, & Mementos

Campsite Log

Dates: .... Address/location: ....

Traveling from: .... Travel mileage: .... Time to destination: ....

Notable landmarks/sites en route: ....

Driving notes: ....

....

Campground/RV park name: .... Campsite #: ....

Phone number/website: ....

Would stay at this campground again? Y / N   Would stay at this campsite again? Y / N

Site hookups: Water ⬭   Electricity ⬭   Sewer ⬭   Dry camping ⬭   Was site level? Y / N

Site amenities: Cable ⬭   Internet ⬭   Fire pit ⬭   Grill ⬭   Picnic table ⬭

Cell signal at campsite (1 = terrible, 5 = fantastic):   1 2 3 4 5   Carrier: ....

Campground amenities: General store ⬭   Laundry ⬭   Pool ⬭   Bathrooms ⬭

Showers ⬭   Dog park ⬭   Clubhouse ⬭   Dump station ⬭   Restaurant ⬭

Additional campsite notes (noise level, maneuverability, cost, scenery, etc.): ....

....

....

....

Weather during stay: ....

....

Nearby grocery stores and restaurants:

Nearby activities:

New friends and acquaintances:

Notes, Memories, & Mementos

Campsite Log

Dates: .... Address/location: ....

Traveling from: .... Travel mileage: .... Time to destination: ....

Notable landmarks/sites en route: ....

Driving notes: ....

....

Campground/RV park name: .... Campsite #: ....

Phone number/website: ....

Would stay at this campground again? Y / N   Would stay at this campsite again? Y / N

Site hookups: Water ⬚   Electricity ⬚   Sewer ⬚   Dry camping ⬚   Was site level? Y / N

Site amenities: Cable ⬚   Internet ⬚   Fire pit ⬚   Grill ⬚   Picnic table ⬚

Cell signal at campsite (1 = terrible, 5 = fantastic):   1 2 3 4 5   Carrier: ....

Campground amenities: General store ⬚   Laundry ⬚   Pool ⬚   Bathrooms ⬚

              Showers ⬚   Dog park ⬚   Clubhouse ⬚   Dump station ⬚   Restaurant ⬚

Additional campsite notes (noise level, maneuverability, cost, scenery, etc.):

....

....

....

Weather during stay: ....

....

Nearby grocery stores and restaurants:

Nearby activities:

New friends and acquaintances:

Notes, Memories, & Mementos

Campsite Log

Dates: .... Address/location: ....

Traveling from: .... Travel mileage: .... Time to destination: ....

Notable landmarks/sites en route: ....

Driving notes: ....

....

Campground/RV park name: .... Campsite #: ....

Phone number/website: ....

Would stay at this campground again? Y / N   Would stay at this campsite again? Y / N

Site hookups: Water ⬭   Electricity ⬭   Sewer ⬭   Dry camping ⬭   Was site level? Y / N

Site amenities: Cable ⬭   Internet ⬭   Fire pit ⬭   Grill ⬭   Picnic table ⬭

Cell signal at campsite (1 = terrible, 5 = fantastic):   1 2 3 4 5   Carrier: ....

Campground amenities: General store ⬭   Laundry ⬭   Pool ⬭   Bathrooms ⬭

Showers ⬭   Dog park ⬭   Clubhouse ⬭   Dump station ⬭   Restaurant ⬭

Additional campsite notes (noise level, maneuverability, cost, scenery, etc.): ....

....

....

....

Weather during stay: ....

....

Nearby grocery stores and restaurants:

Nearby activities:

New friends and acquaintances:

Notes, Memories, & Mementos

Campsite Log

Dates: .... Address/location: ....

Traveling from: .... Travel mileage: .... Time to destination: ....

Notable landmarks/sites en route: ....

Driving notes: ....

....

Campground/RV park name: .... Campsite #: ....

Phone number/website: ....

Would stay at this campground again? Y / N   Would stay at this campsite again? Y / N

Site hookups: Water ☐   Electricity ☐   Sewer ☐   Dry camping ☐   Was site level? Y / N

Site amenities: Cable ☐   Internet ☐   Fire pit ☐   Grill ☐   Picnic table ☐

Cell signal at campsite (1 = terrible, 5 = fantastic):   1 2 3 4 5   Carrier: ....

Campground amenities: General store ☐   Laundry ☐   Pool ☐   Bathrooms ☐

Showers ☐   Dog park ☐   Clubhouse ☐   Dump station ☐   Restaurant ☐

Additional campsite notes (noise level, maneuverability, cost, scenery, etc.): ....

....

....

....

Weather during stay: ....

....

Nearby grocery stores and restaurants:

Nearby activities:

New friends and acquaintances:

Notes, Memories, & Mementos

Campsite Log

Dates: .... Address/location: ....

Traveling from: .... Travel mileage: .... Time to destination: ....

Notable landmarks/sites en route: ....

Driving notes: ....

....

Campground/RV park name: .... Campsite #: ....

Phone number/website: ....

Would stay at this campground again? Y / N   Would stay at this campsite again? Y / N

Site hookups: Water ⬜   Electricity ⬜   Sewer ⬜   Dry camping ⬜   Was site level? Y / N

Site amenities: Cable ⬜   Internet ⬜   Fire pit ⬜   Grill ⬜   Picnic table ⬜

Cell signal at campsite (1 = terrible, 5 = fantastic):   1   2   3   4   5   Carrier: ....

Campground amenities: General store ⬜   Laundry ⬜   Pool ⬜   Bathrooms ⬜

          Showers ⬜   Dog park ⬜   Clubhouse ⬜   Dump station ⬜   Restaurant ⬜

Additional campsite notes (noise level, maneuverability, cost, scenery, etc.): ....

....

....

....

Weather during stay: ....

....

Nearby grocery stores and restaurants:

Nearby activities:

New friends and acquaintances:

Notes, Memories, & Mementos

Campsite Log

Dates: .... Address/location: ....

Traveling from: .... Travel mileage: .... Time to destination: ....

Notable landmarks/sites en route: ....

Driving notes: ....

....

Campground/RV park name: .... Campsite #: ....

Phone number/website: ....

Would stay at this campground again? Y / N   Would stay at this campsite again? Y / N

Site hookups: Water ⬡   Electricity ⬡   Sewer ⬡   Dry camping ⬡   Was site level? Y / N

Site amenities: Cable ⬡   Internet ⬡   Fire pit ⬡   Grill ⬡   Picnic table ⬡

Cell signal at campsite (1 = terrible, 5 = fantastic):   1 2 3 4 5   Carrier: ....

Campground amenities: General store ⬡   Laundry ⬡   Pool ⬡   Bathrooms ⬡

          Showers ⬡   Dog park ⬡   Clubhouse ⬡   Dump station ⬡   Restaurant ⬡

Additional campsite notes (noise level, maneuverability, cost, scenery, etc.): ....

....

....

....

Weather during stay: ....

....

Nearby grocery stores and restaurants:

Nearby activities:

New friends and acquaintances:

Notes, Memories, & Mementos

Campsite Log

Dates: .... Address/location: ....

Traveling from: .... Travel mileage: .... Time to destination: ....

Notable landmarks/sites en route: ....

Driving notes: ....

....

Campground/RV park name: .... Campsite #: ....

Phone number/website: ....

Would stay at this campground again? Y / N   Would stay at this campsite again? Y / N

Site hookups: Water 🔲   Electricity 🔲   Sewer 🔲   Dry camping 🔲   Was site level? Y / N

Site amenities: Cable 🔲   Internet 🔲   Fire pit 🔲   Grill 🔲   Picnic table 🔲

Cell signal at campsite (1 = terrible, 5 = fantastic):   1 2 3 4 5   Carrier: ....

Campground amenities: General store 🔲   Laundry 🔲   Pool 🔲   Bathrooms 🔲

Showers 🔲   Dog park 🔲   Clubhouse 🔲   Dump station 🔲   Restaurant 🔲

Additional campsite notes (noise level, maneuverability, cost, scenery, etc.): ....

....

....

....

Weather during stay: ....

....

Nearby grocery stores and restaurants:

Nearby activities:

New friends and acquaintances:

Notes, Memories, & Mementos

Campsite Log

Dates: .... Address/location: ....

Traveling from: .... Travel mileage: .... Time to destination: ....

Notable landmarks/sites en route: ....

Driving notes: ....

....

Campground/RV park name: .... Campsite #: ....

Phone number/website: ....

Would stay at this campground again? Y / N   Would stay at this campsite again? Y / N

Site hookups: Water ◯   Electricity ◯   Sewer ◯   Dry camping ◯   Was site level? Y / N

Site amenities: Cable ◯   Internet ◯   Fire pit ◯   Grill ◯   Picnic table ◯

Cell signal at campsite (1 = terrible, 5 = fantastic):   1 2 3 4 5   Carrier: ....

Campground amenities: General store ◯   Laundry ◯   Pool ◯   Bathrooms ◯

          Showers ◯   Dog park ◯   Clubhouse ◯   Dump station ◯   Restaurant ◯

Additional campsite notes (noise level, maneuverability, cost, scenery, etc.): ....

....

....

....

Weather during stay: ....

....

Nearby grocery stores and restaurants:

Nearby activities:

New friends and acquaintances:

Notes, Memories, & Mementos

Campsite Log

Dates: .... Address/location: ....

Traveling from: .... Travel mileage: .... Time to destination: ....

Notable landmarks/sites en route: ....

Driving notes: ....

....

Campground/RV park name: .... Campsite #: ....

Phone number/website: ....

Would stay at this campground again? Y / N   Would stay at this campsite again? Y / N

Site hookups: Water ⬡   Electricity ⬡   Sewer ⬡   Dry camping ⬡   Was site level? Y / N

Site amenities: Cable ⬡   Internet ⬡   Fire pit ⬡   Grill ⬡   Picnic table ⬡

Cell signal at campsite (1 = terrible, 5 = fantastic):   1 2 3 4 5   Carrier: ....

Campground amenities: General store ⬡   Laundry ⬡   Pool ⬡   Bathrooms ⬡

          Showers ⬡   Dog park ⬡   Clubhouse ⬡   Dump station ⬡   Restaurant ⬡

Additional campsite notes (noise level, maneuverability, cost, scenery, etc.): ....

....

....

....

Weather during stay: ....

....

Nearby grocery stores and restaurants:

Nearby activities:

New friends and acquaintances:

Notes, Memories, & Mementos

Campsite Log

Dates: .... Address/location: ....

Traveling from: .... Travel mileage: .... Time to destination: ....

Notable landmarks/sites en route: ....

Driving notes: ....

....

Campground/RV park name: .... Campsite #: ....

Phone number/website: ....

Would stay at this campground again? Y / N   Would stay at this campsite again? Y / N

Site hookups: Water ⬭   Electricity ⬭   Sewer ⬭   Dry camping ⬭   Was site level? Y / N

Site amenities: Cable ⬭   Internet ⬭   Fire pit ⬭   Grill ⬭   Picnic table ⬭

Cell signal at campsite (1 = terrible, 5 = fantastic):   1 2 3 4 5   Carrier: ....

Campground amenities: General store ⬭   Laundry ⬭   Pool ⬭   Bathrooms ⬭

Showers ⬭   Dog park ⬭   Clubhouse ⬭   Dump station ⬭   Restaurant ⬭

Additional campsite notes (noise level, maneuverability, cost, scenery, etc.):
....

....

....

....

Weather during stay: ....

....

Nearby grocery stores and restaurants:

Nearby activities:

New friends and acquaintances:

Notes, Memories, & Mementos

site

50

Campsite Log

Dates: .... Address/location: ....

Traveling from: .... Travel mileage: .... Time to destination: ....

Notable landmarks/sites en route: ....

Driving notes: ....

....

Campground/RV park name: .... Campsite #: ....

Phone number/website: ....

Would stay at this campground again? Y / N   Would stay at this campsite again? Y / N

Site hookups: Water ⬡   Electricity ⬡   Sewer ⬡   Dry camping ⬡   Was site level? Y / N

Site amenities: Cable ⬡   Internet ⬡   Fire pit ⬡   Grill ⬡   Picnic table ⬡

Cell signal at campsite (1 = terrible, 5 = fantastic):   1 2 3 4 5   Carrier: ....

Campground amenities: General store ⬡   Laundry ⬡   Pool ⬡   Bathrooms ⬡

Showers ⬡   Dog park ⬡   Clubhouse ⬡   Dump station ⬡   Restaurant ⬡

Additional campsite notes (noise level, maneuverability, cost, scenery, etc.): ....

....

....

....

Weather during stay: ....

....

Nearby grocery stores and restaurants:

Nearby activities:

New friends and acquaintances:

Notes, Memories, & Mementos

Total Mileage Logs

Record the starting location, ending location, mileage, and drive time between each destination to track how many miles and hours you spent on the road during that leg of your trip. At the end of the entire trip, add up the mileage and hours columns to determine the total length and time of the full road trip.

Date	Starting Location	Odometer Start	Departure Time	Ending Location	Odometer Finish	Arrival Time	Mileage	Hours
Total Mileage and Hours Driven for the Entire Trip:								

Date	Starting Location	Odometer Start	Departure Time	Ending Location	Odometer Finish	Arrival Time	Mileage	Hours
Total Mileage and Hours Driven for the Entire Trip:								

Date	Starting Location	Odometer Start	Departure Time	Ending Location	Odometer Finish	Arrival Time	Mileage	Hours
Total Mileage and Hours Driven for the Entire Trip:								

Date	Starting Location	Odometer Start	Departure Time	Ending Location	Odometer Finish	Arrival Time	Mileage	Hours
Total Mileage and Hours Driven for the Entire Trip:								

Date	Starting Location	Odometer Start	Departure Time	Ending Location	Odometer Finish	Arrival Time	Mileage	Hours
Total Mileage and Hours Driven for the Entire Trip:								

RV Maintenance and Repair Log

Date Serviced	Vehicle Serviced	Serviced By	Cost	Description of Work

RV Maintenance and Repair Log

Date Serviced	Vehicle Serviced	Serviced By	Cost	Description of Work

PART 3

Trip Favorites and Memories

Remembering Your Trip

Your trip may be over, but there's no need to forget the good times! Before putting down this travel journal, take some time to reflect on some of your overall favorites from the trip—the best stories, campgrounds, and sights. You can even record some of the difficult moments; those just might end up being some of the memories you'll cherish.

Favorites

Favorite Campgrounds/RV Parks/Camping Spots

Favorite Campsites

Favorite Meals

....

....

....

....

....

Favorite Animals Seen on the Trip

....

....

....

....

....

....

Most Beautiful Drives

Favorite Roadside Stops or Attractions

Favorite Campfire Experiences

....

....

....

....

....

Favorite Scenic Views

....

....

....

....

....

Memories from the Trip

Funniest Moments

....

....

....

....

....

Most Surprising Moments

....

....

....

....

....

Most Difficult Moments

Favorite Overall Moments and Experiences

Favorite Overall Moments and Experiences (Continued)

Ideas for the Next Trip

Now that you've finished this trip, where do you want to go next? Use this space to dream and plan your next big adventure!